T0080372

FIGHTING GAME ESPORTS

THE COMPETITIVE GAMING WORLD OF SUPER SMASH BROS., STREET FIGHTER, AND MORE!

by Thomas Kingsley Troupe

CAPSTONE PRESS
a capstone imprint

Edge Books are published by Capstone Press,
1710 Roe Crest Drive, North Mankato, Minnesota 56003
www.capstonepub.com

Library of Congress Cataloging-in-Publication Data
Names: Troupe, Thomas Kingsley, author.
Title: Fighting game esports : the competitive gaming world of Super Smash
    Bros., Street fighter, and more! / by Thomas Kingsley Troupe.
Description: North Mankato, Minnesota : Capstone Press, 2020. | Series: Edge
    books. Wide world of esports | Includes bibliographical references and index. |
    Audience: Age 8–14. | Audience: Grade 4 to 6.
Identifiers: LCCN 2019005958 (print) | LCCN 2019006601 (ebook) |
    ISBN 9781543573671 (eBook PDF) | ISBN 9781543573558 (library hardcover) |
    ISBN 9781543574548 (paperback)
Subjects: LCSH: Video games—Competitions—Juvenile literature. | Video
    gamers—Juvenile literature.
Classification: LCC GV1469.3 (ebook) | LCC GV1469.3 .T768 2020 (print) |
    DDC 794.8—dc23
LC record available at https://lccn.loc.gov/2019005958

Summary: Describes the history of professional video gaming and game
tournaments including *Super Smash Bros.*, *Street Fighter*, *Dragon Ball FighterZ*,
and others.

Editorial Credits
Aaron Sautter, editor; Kyle Grenz, designer; Tracy Cummins, media researcher;
Laura Manthe, production specialist

Photo Credits
Alamy: Ken Howard, 6-7; Getty Images: CHANDAN KHANNA/AFP, 21, Daniel
Shirey, 14, GREG BAKER/AFP, 22-23, Joe Buglewicz, 17, 18, 24, 28, UNG YEON-
JE/AFP, 10-11; iStockphoto: adamkaz, 26; Newscom: Kyodo, 5; Reuters Pictures:
Elijah Nouvelage, 12-13; Shutterstock: aslysun, 20, Daniel Fung, Design Element,
dwphotos, 4, EKKAPHAN CHIMPALEE, Design Element, Eky Studio, Design
Element, Eugene Adebari, 9, glazok90, Design Element, Gorodenkoff, Cover Top
Left, Cover Top Right, Leonel Calara, 27, Maryna Kulchytska, Design Element,
Phojai Phanpanya, Design Element, Rvector, Design Element, Sevastsyanau
Uladzimir, 29; Wikimedia: Flickr/Joi Ito, 8

All internet sites listed in the back matter were accurate and available at the time
this book was published.

Printed in the United States   5863

Table of
Contents

CHAPTER 1

READY? FIGHT!

You stand in the middle of the village square, your fists up in preparation. All around you, eyes are watching and waiting for you to make your move. The ends of the **bandanna** tied around your head blow in the breeze. You look your opponent in the eye, and he sneers back. You rock back and forth on your legs, trying to loosen up. It won't be long now.

bandanna—a large, brightly colored handkerchief

Street Fighter V is known for its intense fighting action and the characters' special moves.

Somewhere in the crowd, a loud voice shouts: ROUND 1! FIGHT! You immediately rush at your opponent. He spins and launches a high kick that barely misses your head. You crouch and punch him in the mid-section, knocking him backward. As he recovers, you leap into the air and catch his chin with a strong **uppercut**. But as you land he sweeps your feet and knocks you down. When you get up, you see your enemy forming a magical fireball in his cupped hands. You only have a split second to react. How will you defend yourself?

uppercut—a strong, upward-swinging punch, usually to hit an opponent's chin

Controller Combat

No worries! You're safe behind your controller. So when the fireball hits, you don't feel a thing. But you do hear the roar of the crowd. Much like fans at a real-life wrestling match, the crowd cheers with every blow. When your opponent's fighter suddenly leaps, you rapidly punch in a wicked button combination. On the screen, your character launches a flaming uppercut, catching the enemy in mid-air. The crowd goes crazy as both fighters' health bars are slowly chipped away. It's going to be a close match. Who will be the last one standing?

Just as real fighting competitions draw thousands of fans, so does the esports fighting game craze. The popularity of competitive video gaming has grown at an amazing rate in recent years. Thousands of fighting game fans pack arenas to cheer on their favorite players. Meanwhile, millions more tune in around the world to watch the big matches online.

Pro gamer "Infiltration" faced off against "Fuudo" in the *Street Fighter V* Finals at the Evolution (EVO) 2016 Championships held in Las Vegas, Nevada.

But it's not just the adoring crowds that draw players to the professional esports scene. Gamers can often earn a good living by turning pro. Glory, fame, and fortune await those few who win a championship. In the competitive world of esport fighting tournaments, there can be only one!

CHAPTER 2

Spacewar!

ESPORT ORIGINS

Old School Showdowns

Would you believe that the first esports competition happened nearly 50 years ago? It's true. In 1972 some computer programmers at Stanford University held the first Intergalactic Spacewar Olympics. *Spacewar!* was a very simple game compared to the games of today. Each player controlled a small ship and fired weapons at their opponent. Players also had to stay away from the sun in the middle of the screen. The tournament winner, Stewart Brand, became the first-ever esports champion.

FUN FACT

Spacewar! went through many changes after it was created in 1962. New features were added to make the game more fun. These included cloaking devices, space bombs, and the ability to add more players on the screen at once.

In the earliest esport competitions, space games were very popular. In 1980 the Atari video game company put together a tournament featuring its most popular game, *Space Invaders*. The competition drew more than 10,000 players across several major U.S. cities. The tournament was featured in newspapers and on TV. The idea that people could play video games competitively quickly caught on among gaming fans.

FUN FACT

Space Invaders was both a popular arcade game and a game that could be played at home. Gamers who had an Atari 2600 game system at their house could practice up before the big tournament!

Online Opponents

In the 1990s the internet became incredibly popular, and so did competitive online gaming. Gamers soon began competing against each other across great distances. As more and more people logged on to do battle, game companies saw a great chance to boost their game sales. Companies began to **sponsor** video game tournaments to find out which gamers were the best of the best.

One large online competition got its start in South Korea. In the 1990s many internet cafes sprang up around the country. Young people spent a lot of time at these small shops to get their fill of online gaming. Many players competed in a space strategy game called *StarCraft*. The game became so popular that online matches were broadcast on Korean TV. The game soon developed into an incredibly popular esports league. The StarCraft series is still so popular in South Korea that some players have made playing the game into a career. Some players make over $100,000 a year playing the game!

sponsor—to provide money or equipment for a player or team in exchange for advertising

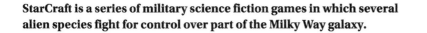

StarCraft is a series of military science fiction games in which several alien species fight for control over part of the Milky Way galaxy.

FUN FACT

The game *Quake* was the main attraction of the Red Annihilation Tournament. In 1997 players converged on Atlanta, Georgia, to face off in the finals. The champion of the tournament won $5,000 and a custom Ferrari 328 GTS. The Red Annihilation Tournament is considered by many to be the first official esports competition.

Esports Evolution

In the 2000s and early 2010s, esports competitions continued to grow in popularity. To meet the rising interest, Twitch.tv was created in 2011. Twitch streams video of games to fans through the internet. When the site began live-streaming esports competitions, its popularity exploded. During the service's first year, it averaged about 100,000 people watching at any one time. In early 2019 that average had grown to more than 1.2 million viewers.

Proletariat_Inc playing Board Games

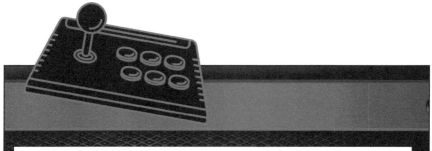

Record Viewers

Millions of viewers from all over the world tune in to watch esports competitions. So far, the record for most watched esports event took place in 2018 for the Mid-Season Invitational final. The *League of Legends* championship match featured finalists from China and Korea. More than 127 million fans tuned in to watch!

Twitch.tv offers viewers thousands of channels of live content to choose from at any time.

One of the most exciting parts of esports competitions are the prizes. As tournament viewership grew, so did the number of sponsors paying to advertise during the events. This growth in income helped drive up the prize money that esport champions could take home. Today, esports has become a big business. By the year 2020, competitions are expected to create more than $1.5 billion in **revenue**.

revenue—the money that is made by a business

Victor "Punk" Woodley faced Arman "Phenom" Hanjani in the Grand Final of the 2017 ELEAGUE Street Fighter V Invitational.

GET IN THE RING!

Street Fighter Competitions

One of the biggest fighting game tournaments today is the ELEAGUE Street Fighter V Invitational. ELEAGUE invites 32 of the world's top players to compete. The first 16 players are chosen based on their performance at pro tour competitions. Capcom, the company that created the Street Fighter series, invites the other 16 players.

The tournament is set up in a **bracket** style. Four groups of eight players compete to get to the playoffs. During the playoffs, groups of two players compete against one another in each round. The first player to win three out of five games advances to the next round. Play continues this way until the final two players face off in the championship match.

Street Survivor

In 2018 Turner Broadcasting created a reality-based program called *ELEAGUE: The Challenger.* The show featured seven *Street Fighter V* pros living under the same roof. One player was eliminated each week through a series of gaming challenges. The final player earned a spot in the ELEAGUE Street Fighter V Invitational tournament and a chance to win the $150,000 grand prize.

FUN FACT

The 2018 winner from the ELEAGUE Street Fighter V Invitational took home $150,000 from the $250,000 prize pool. The champion was Hajime Taniguchi Tokido (gamertag: Tokido) who defeated Bryant Huggins (gamertag: Smug).

1st	US$150,000
2nd	US$40,000
3rd	US$20,000
4th	US$12,000
5th – 6th	US$5,000
7th – 8th	US$3,000
9th – 16th	US$1,000
17th – 24th	US$500
25th – 32nd	US$0

bracket—a way to organize players or teams in a tournament; as they win they advance through the bracket to the championship game

Super Smash Competitions

One of the newest game series featured in ELEAGUE fighting is Super Smash Bros. With the release of Nintendo's *Super Smash Bros. Ultimate*, the company began to see the potential of the esports arena. Nintendo's newest game in the franchise was featured in the first Super Smash Bros. Ultimate Invitational.

The tournament featured eight casual and pro gamers competing against each other. To make things interesting, some rounds saw players teaming up with opponents in two-on-two competitions. Each player picked three of the more than 70 characters in the game. Each character had to be used at least once, so players had to think carefully about which character to use in each round.

FUN FACT

The object of the game in Super Smash Bros. isn't to knock the opponents "out," but rather to knock them "off." The fight takes place on a stage. As the characters take damage, they are more likely to be knocked off the stage and lose that match.

The bracket itself was like an obstacle course of competition. The first round was set up as doubles matches. The winners then played against their partners in the second round. The winners of those matches then faced each other in the finals until one was crowned the *Super Smash Bros. Ultimate* champion.

William "Leffen" Hjelte (right) won the *Super Smash Bros. Melee* singles title at EVO 2018.

Dragon Ball FighterZ World Tour

Another exciting fighting game in the esports world is *Dragon Ball FighterZ*. Based on the popular Japanese animé series, the game's graphics look like they were lifted directly from the cartoon.

Ryota "Kazunoko" Inoue (right) dominated the Dragon Ball FighterZ World Tour, winning four out of seven possible dragon balls to reach the Finals.

The Dragon Ball FighterZ World Tour is an eight-month tournament series. Players from around the world compete in one-on-one combat at each event. Players are awarded a "Dragon Ball" for winning or placing in the tournaments. The more Dragon Balls a player receives, the better **seed** they have in the World Tour Finals. The finals competition uses a **double elimination** format. Players have to lose twice to be removed from competition. Players who lose in the first round can still make it to the championship. However, they have to keep winning to make it to the final round.

The 2018 Dragon Ball FighterZ World Tour winner was Kazunoko, who had beaten Fenritti in the first round. But Fenritti fought his way through the losers bracket, earning a chance to face off against Kazunoko in the Grand Finals. Sadly, he lost again. Fenritti wasn't the Grand Champion, but he still won 2nd place and $5,000.

FUN FACT

Esports tournaments aren't only streamed online. Fans can also watch competitions broadcast on ESPN, just like other sports.

double elimination—a type of competition in which a team or player must lose twice to be eliminated

seed—how a team is ranked for a playoff tournament

CHAPTER 4

TRAIN HARD TO PLAY HARD

Turning a love of games into a career sounds like the dream job. Just pick up your controller and put in a full day of gaming bliss. But the truth is professional esport athletes need to train like any other athletes. And it isn't always as fun as it might sound.

Esport pros usually have a grueling training schedule. Ever get sick of playing the same game after an hour or two? Imagine playing it for 10 hours or more every day! The pros put in hundreds of hours of practice so they know every possible punch, kick, and special move.

Esport gamers often work with coaches too. Coaches watch players and teach them how to play better, faster, and smarter. They also study videos of upcoming opponents to find any weaknesses and plan strategy. With a coach's help, players hope to gain an edge to claim the championship.

Esport pro gamers put in long hours of training and practice so they are ready to compete with the best.

Training for the Big Time

For some esport athletes, practicing on their own or even with a coach isn't always enough. Fighting games are loaded with special moves, combos, and strategies for each game character. To become the best, serious esports hopefuls can join fighting game schools, or **dojos**. There, players can train with the best instructors and learn how to conquer the esports fighting arena.

It's a lot of hard work, but the players that rise to the top can earn great rewards. The average salary for a pro esports athlete is about $60,000 a year. And if they can earn sponsorships and start winning big events, that number can skyrocket quickly. Some of the highest paid gamers earn about $180,000 per year—before winning any prize money at tournaments!

dojo—a school where students learn to fight in hand-to-hand combat, often using martial arts

Serious pro gamers often work with coaches or take special esports classes to learn new strategies and improve their skills.

FUN FACT

Have you ever been told that playing video games is bad for you? That's not entirely true. Studies have shown that surgeons who play video games often do their jobs faster and make fewer mistakes than those who don't play. Power up, doctor!

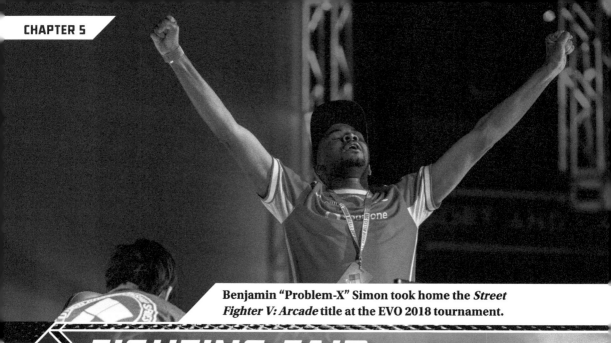

CHAPTER 5

Benjamin "Problem-X" Simon took home the *Street Fighter V: Arcade* title at the EVO 2018 tournament.

FIGHTING FAIR

Every year millions of fans around the world tune in to watch their favorite games and gamers. With esports being so popular, becoming a pro player seems like something that just about anyone could do. However, esport competitions seem to be dominated by white and Asian gamers. With so many opportunities, why are there so few black or Latino people in the pro gaming scene?

Unfortunately, racist attitudes are not uncommon in the gaming world. During the heat of battle, some fans and players let their emotions take over. And some of them might make hurtful or racist remarks.

Thankfully, most pro gaming leagues are working hard to discourage this type of behavior. Pro players who use hateful language can be fined or even ejected from the tournaments. While these actions can't solve all the problems of inclusion in esports, it's a step in the right direction.

Money Train

Pro gamers earn a lot of money and huge cash prizes are handed out at tournaments. Where does all the money in esports come from?

Sponsorships:

Sponsors often financially support pro players and major tournaments so they can get free advertising for their products.

Advertising:

Companies often pay for commercial time to advertise their products to the millions of people watching at home.

Media Rights:

Websites and TV channels often pay esport leagues to stream or broadcast live games.

Game Publisher Fees:

Many game publishers pay fees to have their games used in tournaments.

Tickets and Merchandise:

Esport leagues make a lot of money from selling tickets and souvenirs to fans at large events.

Women in Esports

Racism is a big enough problem in esports. But there's also a shortage of professional female esport players. Playing video games was once considered to be a male-only activity. For a long time, people felt that women and girls shouldn't play games, especially competing alongside professional male players. For this reason, some women have experienced verbal abuse from sexist competitors and fans.

Tournament organizers are trying to change those hurtful attitudes and behaviors. They are working to encourage more women to compete in the esports community. Some have even started organizing female-centric tournaments. Competitions like the Girl Gamer Esports Festival highlight women in gaming and offer environments where gender equality is valued.

"Sherryjenix" Nhan took on "DSC Sgt Slap" in a *Street Fighter V* match at the 2016 NCR NorCal Regionals tournament.

ATHLETE OR NOT?

One of the biggest challenges esports pros face is the idea of respect. Most people don't consider pro gamers to be true athletes. Instead, they just see someone playing video games. Part of the problem is the belief that gamers are lazy and have little interest in anything else. Some argue that true sports require physical movement and sweat. But others argue that hand-to-eye coordination and physical dexterity are also things that great athletes use a lot. Not everyone will agree that competitive gaming is a sport. But there's no arguing that esports draw audiences rivaling the biggest "real" pro sports events.

Thousands of fans packed the arena to watch the *Dragon Ball FighterZ* Finals during EVO 2018 in Las Vegas, Nevada.

Ready to Rumble?

Esports is like a snowball rolling down the side of a snowy mountain. Over the years the tournaments have grown into a billion dollar business. Playing video games is no longer just a fun activity people do with their friends. Through esports, gamers have found a way to earn a living with their favorite pastime. And the best players are able to win great fame and fortune.

Even some high schools are getting into the esports craze. The National Federation of State High Schools (NFHS) organizes gaming competitions for students. Currently more than 19,000 schools participate and are introducing students to the world of competitive gaming. Tomorrow's major esport athletes are already training for the big time!

Ready to step in and take your chances in the ring? Then you'll need to grab your controller and practice, practice, practice. Pick your best fighter and perfect those combos. Then brace yourself for a fast-paced slugfest as you fight your way to the top!

Glossary

bandanna (ban-DAN-uh)—a large, brightly colored handkerchief

bracket (BRAK-it)—a way to organize players or teams in a tournament; as they win they advance through the bracket to the championship game

dojo (DOH-joh)—a school where students learn to fight in hand-to-hand combat, often using martial arts

double elimination (DUH-buhl i-li-muh-NAY-shuhn)—a type of competition in which a team or player must lose twice to be eliminated

revenue (REV-uh-noo)—the money that is made by a business

seed (SEED)—how a team is ranked for a playoff tournament

sponsor (SPON-sur)—to provide money or equipment for a player or team in exchange for advertising

uppercut (UHP-er-kuht)—a strong, upward-swinging punch, usually to hit an opponent's chin

Read More

Jankowski, Matthew. *The Modern Nerd's Guide to eSports*. Geek Out! New York: Gareth Stevens Publishing, 2018.

Marquardt, Meg. *Women in E-Sports*. E-Sports: Game On! Chicago: Norwood House Press, 2019.

Mauleón, Daniel. *Esports Revolution*. Video Game Revolution. North Mankato, MN: Capstone Press, 2020.

Internet Sites

ESPN—Esports
http://www.espn.com/esports/

Esports Earnings
https://www.esportsearnings.com/

Esports History
https://www.hotspawn.com/the-history-of-esports/

Index